Why is Saying Goodbye So Hard?

COPING
WITH THE DEATH
OF A PET

ERIN DOLORES BAMBERY

Why Is Saying Goodbye So Hard?
Copyright © 2021 by Erin Bambery

First Edition

Paperback ISBN: 978-1-63837-994-2

DEDICATION

This book is dedicated to anyone
who has felt the loss of a furry friend.
Special thanks to the families
of the late pets that appear in this book.

Bowie (front cover, pages 1, 14 & 21)

Hammy (page 5)

Furry Durry (page 6)

Bo (page 9)

Reepicheep (page 10)

Lelu (page 11)

Cilla (page 13)

Layna (page 16)

Nugget (page 17)

Duncan (page 18)

Having a pet is like having a best friend that lives with you all the time.

Some pets are older when they come home, and some are just babies.

You might notice that your pet grows much faster than you do. This is because pets have shorter lives than people. Having less time makes every moment all the more special with your furry friend.

When a pet has lived a long time, and becomes very old, you might start to see some changes in them. They might sleep more and eat less. Your pet might not be as active as they used to be. Sometimes pets get sick and are not able to get better.

It's always sad when a pet's time is up
and they pass away. Sometimes it is a
surprise when pets die, and other times
we can see signs of their lives ending.
If a pet is sick or in pain, their family
might decide to put them to sleep.

This is something that is done by a veterinarian. They help pets pass away in a peaceful, painless way so that they will not suffer anymore.

After a pet dies, there are a few different things that can happen to their body. Some people bury their pets and others have them cremated.

Being cremated means that the pet's body will be turned into ashes. People usually put these ashes in a small jar called an urn. Sometimes the pet's body does not come back to their family and that is ok too. It is important to remember that your pet has passed away and they can no longer feel any sickness or pain.

When your pet dies it is normal to feel very, very sad. This sadness is called grief. You might be reminded of your pet by things in your house that belonged to them or pictures of them. It is ok to be upset by this. It means that your pet was an important part of your life.

Crying about your pet dying is normal and can help you let your feelings out. Many people are also helped by talking to friends, family, or counselors about their grief.

A pet dying can be just as difficult to deal with as a person dying. Some people don't understand this and may say things like "it's just an animal." These people are not trying to be mean; they just don't have the same feelings about your pet as you do and that is ok.

It is important to remember that once a pet has passed away, they will not come back. This is particularly hard for people who were not able to say goodbye, or people who wanted to spend more time with their pets than they were able to. Some people feel better by writing down what they wanted to say to their pets in a journal, or even as a letter to them.

Nobody knows for sure what happens when pets and people die. Many people feel better by thinking about their pet being in Heaven with the angels. Sometimes people feel like their pet is watching over them and still loving them, just in a different way. People sometimes feel better by praying and asking God to take care of their pet while they are in Heaven. Sometimes people pray to let their pet know that they love and miss them. Even though your pet cannot contact you anymore, it can help to know that they are still listening.

People can feel guilty that they did not spend enough time with their pet before they died. This is normal and almost everyone feels this way when their pet dies. Your pet knows that you love them. It can help to remind yourself of all the time that you DID spend with them and how happy you both were.

As time goes on it will become easier to deal with the grief of losing your friend. While the sadness can be overwhelming at first, you will start to feel better eventually and be less upset when thinking about your pet.

Starting to feel better does not mean that you miss your pet any less. It just means that you have accepted that they are gone and can think about how happy you were when your pet was here, instead of how sad it is to be apart.

If you are having a really difficult time accepting your pet's death or are not feeling better after a long time, it is a good idea to tell your parents, a teacher, a school counselor, or another trusted adult. Losing a friend is really hard and there are people who can help you through it.

So when is it time to get another pet?
The answer is whenever you feel ready.
Some people might want to get another
pet right away because they feel lonely,
but it is important to wait and make sure
that you are able to handle it first.

New pets can often bring back memories of old pets. It is important that being reminded of your old pet no longer upsets you before getting a new one. When, and if, your family decides to get a new pet, try not to think of them as a replacement for the one that passed away. There is room in your heart for as many pets and people as you want. Loving a new pet does not mean you love your deceased pet any less. In fact, giving a wonderful life to another furry friend is a really good way to remember and honor the ones who are no longer with us.

The pets that we love never completely leave us. Their memory stays alive in our hearts forever.

CPSIA information can be obtained
at www.ICGtesting.com
Printed in the USA
BVHW020510011221
622781BV00002B/38